BITCOIN
A How-To Guide
for Small Business

BY **GLEN LEE ROBERTS**
'EARTHLING'

A SPECIAL LIMITED EDITION

ISBN Paperback: 978-99953-2-975-4

ISBN Edition Digital: 978-99953-2-974-7

TABLE OF CONTENTS

1. To Begin With

I have been actively interested in technology, government activities, privacy, and related topics for most of my life, but I was somewhat of a late starter with bitcoin. It wasn't until after I had renounced my US citizenship and become stateless (in June 2013) that I began my bitcoin adventure.

Until the end of 2014, my bitcoin activities were online. Then a restaurant here in Asuncion, Paraguay (Be Okay) where I live, started accepting bitcoin, I loaded up a wallet app on my cell phone and went to have dinner. Then I made a plan to see if I could use bitcoin as the base for my daily living expenses.

That was quite a challenge because there are just a few places that accept bitcoin. However, I was able to obtain a prepaid Mastercard that is refilled with bitcoin. I have now been paying the majority of my daily expenses indirectly via bitcoin. I hope over the next year or two that I will be able to continue that, but pay them directly.

That depends on more local businesses accepting bitcoin. From my point of view the process for a business to accept bitcoin is simple and straightforward. I believe for an investment of approximately $150 you could accept bitcoin via a dedicated point of sale terminal (POS) and a prepaid Mastercard to spend your bitcoin with. However, you can start with a budget of zero.

You could use your current smartphone or PC as the bitcoin POS, and then wait until you have made a few sales and use those proceeds to obtain the prepaid Mastercard, and later a dedicated POS terminal.

When I made the choice to become stateless, to give up my nationality and not take another, I made a choice not to support what I believed was a failed political system (the US). Although I don't have a bond of citizenship to any country, it does not mean I am looking to live a lawless life. It simply means I have more personal responsibility for my actions.

Many refer to bitcoin as a stateless currency. It is not associated with a central bank or political system. Rather than having political leaders or central bankers who manipulate its' value or "control" it in one way or other, bitcoin rests upon mathematical formulas.

By using bitcoin you can achieve two objectives. First, you can be a part of the new economy. Whether bitcoin will be the "currency" of the future or not, can only be answered over the coming years. However, I think it is clear that bitcoin will play a significant role in the transition from the currencies of today into the future. The second aspect of using bitcoin is that by doing nothing more than using it, you will disempower those who have been controlling the money and financial systems for their own purposes.

Look at just the past 40 years of technology; you can see that every year it gets better and better. The engineers, hardware developers, software developers … everyone involved responds to industry and media "feedback," which makes products and services better. Look at the transition from the old "bag phones" to the "smart-phone" of today.

However, look at political systems. It feels as if the opposite is happening. The "feedback" – the voice of the people individually and through the media – falls on deaf ears. The options at the voting booth are futile, possibly described as "worse or worse". The transition looks like a little chaos to more chaos.

Which system do you think can do a better job with your finances? I think that within the realm of virtual currencies we will see the same advancement we've seen with technology. The options, the processes, the technology will get better and better. The feedback loop works.

You can get started today and start to take advantages of the technological and financial benefits of bitcoin in your business starting today.

2. A Bit Regarding Bitcoin

In this chapter, we'll discuss bitcoin from a historical standpoint. Bitcoin is called a "crypto-currency" in that uses digital Internet technology for purposes of creation and dissemination.

The founder of bitcoin is the mysterious Satoshi Nakamoto, who published a paper on the Internet describing how a currency like bitcoin would work. In fact, there is considerable controversy over who he is and even whether he exists. Here's how Wikipedia describes the genesis:

In November 2008, a paper was posted on the internet under the name Satoshi Nakamoto titled Bitcoin: A Peer-to-Peer Electronic Cash System. This paper detailed methods of using a peer-to-peer network to generate what was described as "a system for electronic transactions without relying on trust." In January 2009, the bitcoin network came into existence with the release of the first open source bitcoin client and the issuance of the first bitcoins, with Satoshi Nakamoto mining the first block of bitcoins ever (known as the "genesis block"), which had a reward of 50 bitcoins. The value of the first bitcoin transactions were negotiated by individuals on the bitcointalk forums with one notable transaction of 10,000 BTC used to indirectly purchase two pizzas delivered by Papa John's.

Other purchases followed. Wikileaks announced it would accept bitcoin donations and for a while The Electronic Frontier Foundation (EFF) accepted the currency as well. Later on, the EFF suspended and then re-initiated bitcoin donations. By 2012, BitPay claimed to have 1,000 merchants accepting bitcoin. By February 2013, payment processor Coinbase claimed to have sold US$1 million worth of bitcoins in one month at over $22 per bitcoin.

As Bitcoin gained in popularity, it moved up significantly from a price standpoint, reaching US$1,000 before going back down. The pricing of bitcoin is carried out by bitcoin exchanges that coordinated buying and selling between customers. Some of these exchanges have gone out of business or been faced with accusations of criminality. However, others seem to function quite well.

Bitcoin has continued to gain adherents and naturally been subject to setbacks, with certain bitcoin facilities such as Silk Road being raided and shut down by US law enforcement. Meanwhile, on November 28th, the largest bitcoin exchange, Mr. Gox (located in Japan), valued a single bitcoin at US$1000. Mt. Gox was later shut down by government authorities for financial irregularities.

Today, bitcoin is considered a "virtual currency" by the US and various other Western entities and as such, bitcoin holders have no particular legal obligations.

In the US, the IRS views bitcoin as property; ie: they do not consider the FBAR, FACTA and foreign financial account reporting to apply to Bitcoin accounts. Americans are obligated to report receipts and disbursements of bitcoin as property that was acquired or sold. However, the State of California in 2015 will consider Bitcoin as legal tender.

Bitcoin exchanges where bitcoins are traded for traditional currencies, are under a different set of obligations. According to Wikipedia and other sources, they are, "required to disclose large transactions and suspicious activity, comply with money laundering regulations, and collect information about their customers as traditional financial institutions are required to do."

When it comes to bitcoin, what is important to keep in mind is that users of bitcoin currently are not subject to regulations because the use of bitcoin is currently impossible to regulate. As an encrypted currency, it is does not easily yield itself to any kind of formal tracking.

The weak point when it comes to bitcoin has to do with bitcoin exchanges, which can turn into targets for government snooping and confiscatory gambits. However, when users engage in bitcoin-to-bitcoin transactions between themselves, there is no weak point to expose the transaction to regulatory control.

Bitcoin has also done us the service of illustrating clearly how money is controlled and regulated at a macro level. Many have gained a better understanding of the intersection of money and government power from various official approaches to bitcoin.

The temptation is to believe that extant money systems evolved based on marketplace forces, but government activities directed at bitcoin show us that is decidedly not the case. One method governments use to control money involves creating a broad category of illegal substances and activities. In the modern era, this has revolved in large part around illegal "drugs." Once various behaviors have been made illegal, a host of other activities can be labeled criminal. This is because illegal activities involve money and thus any transaction can be viewed as participating in the initial illegality.

In some cases, things are changing. The United Nations may soon embark on a series of organizational campaigns to legalize and regulate a broad array of drugs. Sex work is slated to become "legal" as well around the world, according to UN sources.

There are various reasons why a consensus if forming around legalizing drugs and sex work, but it is most important to notice that what is "illegal" can be made legal by forming a different official consensus. Viewed within this context, we can see that the law becomes fungible and very obviously represents opportunities for society's controlling factions to create legislative structures that lend themselves to official command-and-control activities, contrary to concepts of liberty as expressed by the constitutions of various countries.

Bitcoin has been attacked because it interferes with this process. It is not trackable or seizeable in the most common sense and thus not easily regulated. And while various efforts have been made to link bitcoin with illegal activities, these are peripheral gambits. The real issue is that bitcoin is an anonymous alternative currency that acts as money.

This may seem odd given that bitcoin is not a precious metal and does not even exist for transaction purposes outside of a computer. Nor is bitcoin the product of monopoly central banking. It is not issued directly out of government mints either.

Bitcoin is private currency. But one can call it money if one wishes, the definition of money being something that people have faith in for transactional purposes and accept as payment.

There are all sorts of theories about what money is and can be, but the most important point is that it is ACCEPTED. Hypothetically there may be reasons why some money is more accepted than others. Gold is said to have "won" the money competition over thousands of years because it is durable, portable, divisible and rare, among other qualities. Bitcoin is certainly not all this. But nonetheless, probably for its anonymity, it has found a favorable market reception.

In many ways, Bitcoin's configuration resembles an earlier kind of money in that it has been generated by the private sector rather than the public one. This is controversial of course, because some monetary historians trace the evolution of money back to temples, which are said to have served as the first banks because they were secure.

The idea here is that money and some sort of community authority are inextricably linked. But this doesn't make much sense within the historical perspective of agriculture, industry and trade generally. Almost always, what becomes established as a government practice begins in the private sector.

Medicine, farming and even metallurgy began privately before being subject to government oversight and regulation. Market-based economic theory explains that the formation of banks and money in the West was influenced by the use of gold and silver, which were often used together as money.

People with gold and silver to store found warehouses to hold their metals. The warehouses offered receipts to customers and eventually customers began to trade the receipts among themselves. Thus "currency" came to be circulated in the community. Eventually warehouses evolved into the banks we know today.

This history deviates from the idea that money was developed under the watchful eyes of priests and their governmental counterparts. But it may be seen as a more natural explanation of how money evolved because it places the private sector in front of the public one.

The evolution of bitcoin has been similar in that it has originated – or seems to have originated – in the private sector. The addition of certain kinds of regulatory oversight follows the historical pattern as well, though one could argue the evolution has been speeded up in this modern era.

The larger issue regarding bitcoin is whether it can remain private money, uncontrolled by regulatory authorities. Many bitcoin enthusiasts envision the evolution of a hybrid system in which portions of bitcoin will be subject to regulation but other portions, critically, will remain beyond the regulatory reach.

Even if bitcoin does at some point become fully regulated, there are many who believe that its ease of use, portability and low transaction costs will support its use and expansion as the world's first, true electronic money.

This perspective is buttressed by a plethora of other electronic coins, all of which are issued privately and are convertible to bitcoin. This evolution seems to show us that bitcoin is not simply an individual phenomenon but is part of a larger electronic revolution that is leading us toward a new kind of monetary future.

3. The Goal

We've learned a little bit about bitcoin, now let's return to the main theme of this book, which is to help local businesses, especially those who are not located within the United States, Europe or Canada to start participating in the bitcoin economy. It should also be helpful for businesses selling online and for independent workers. The different services and processes will also be flagged if they NOT friendly to stateless people or to stateless people without ID.

I should emphasize that to participate in the bitcoin economy nothing more than a bitcoin wallet is necessary. There are no application fees, no application forms, no documents to be verified, no requests for proof of address, nationality or anything else. It is a open financial system truly available to all, and is not controlled by any political entity. It is often referred to as a stateless currency. However, when it interacts with the conventional financial system, then the questions of identification, documents, verification and all the usual banking requires start to rear their ugly heads.

For example, today, at lunch, I ran into two friends and they asked me about bitcoin. I had them install a bitcoin wallet on their cellphones and sent each of them ten cents. In all of five minutes I had two people fully engaged in the bitcoin economy. Imagine trying that at a bank!

I believe ultimately, the bitcoin economy will grow to a point where individuals and businesses will be able to conduct 100% of their financial affairs with bitcoin. That is all their income and purchases can be in bitcoin. The technology for that is here now. The only problem is that as to now, there are only a few places accept bitcoin. You can become one that does.

You can help move the bitcoin economy forward. It won't require any, or no significant investment on your part and you may benefit by instantly developing a network of new customers.

Right now there are few places that you will be able to directly spend income you receive via bitcoin. This book is designed to help bridge that gap. As I start to write this, I have been paying a large percentage of my daily living expenses directly and indirectly with bitcoin. I hope to see the portion of my expenses I can pay directly with bitcoin steadily increase.

This book is not about taxes. Bitcoin, just like dollars, euros, cash, checks, credit cards, and any other form of payment or property may impose various tax obligations on you depending on your nationality, where you live, do business, etc. For those questions, it is best to consult your lawyer and/or accountant. I think the best way to look at bitcoin would be the same as cash.

A restaurant I visit regularly accepts bitcoin. When I ask for the check, I receive the cash register ticket and written at the bottom is the amount in bitcoin. I also get the QR code for sending the bitcoin to. It would appear they account for all their bitcoin sales just the same as a regular cash sale. It's passed through their cash register just as any sale in guaranis (Paraguyan currency) is.

This book will be split into several sections. It will begin by taking you through the steps to accept bitcoin. How you can start doing that within minutes of reading this book. Chapter 11. A Real Transaction Step-by-Step offers a pictorial demonstration of charging a customer in bitcoin and receiving the payment. The book will then progress through some ways that you will be able to use the bitcoin you receive in real life, how to make the checkout process in your establishment smooth, using your bitcoin online and some frequently asked questions. Chapter 12. Quick Bitcoin Wallet Reviews will take a quick look at several options for bitcoin walls.

For the most part the services and processes that I will describe here are based on my personal experiences. Both on the side of receiving bitcoin, but also spending it (directly, and indirectly). For those in the United States, Canada and Europe ("big three areas") the process is exceedingly simply and there is really no excuse for your business not to be accepting bitcoin today.

For those outside those big three areas, I believe once you've read this guide, you'll see that the process is very simple, and that you can start participating in the bitcoin economy without any delay and help increase your sales and be a part of the future today.

4. Bitcoin Addresses, Wallets & Exchanges

The process of accepting bitcoin can be simple or complicated. However, the key is to understand the basics first: bitcoin addresses, wallets and exchanges. A wallet is simply a collection of addresses. An address is simply a destination bitcoin can be sent to. The balance in a wallet is the sum total of all the addresses in the wallet. It is also important to note that while a bitcoin transfer has a destination, it does not have a source.

It is not necessary to understand the big picture, just that unlike other kinds of transfers, there is no clearly defined source. Someone cannot say, "my bitcoin address is xyz, please verify you got my payment". That is one of the reasons why a pure bitcoin implementation would use a single bitcoin address for just a single transaction.

In the most simple form bitcoin is nothing more than presenting someone with a bitcoin address and asking them to send you some bitcoin. Like this: My bitcoin address is
18xVfQuai4hNaoK7vtaW1epCLgejndJcoW
please send me bitcoin. Anyone in the world can send any amount of bitcoin they have to that address.

In the mobile world, there are great difficulties trying to key in that kind of an address and therefore QR codes are commonly used. With your mobile bitcoin wallet (and probably with your webcam on a regular laptop or PC) you can just point it at a QR code and quickly scan in the address. Keep in mind that once you send bitcoin it is sent. You cannot reverse the transaction or complain to the service (there isn't any service or company like with credit cards, Western Union or the like). At best whoever you sent it to could chose to send it back to you. Double check addresses and amounts!

You can scan the QR code at the top of this chapter, and you will see the bitcoin address I have in the text. If you send some bitcoin to that address, I will receive it. The second QR code, although not much different in appearance, also includes an amount. If you scan the second QR code with your bitcoin wallet, it will show the address and the amount of bitcoin as 0.01 bitcoins.

That is how it works in the restaurant I regularly eat and pay with bitcoin. They present me with the check showing the amount in bitcoin and a laminated QR code to scan. I scan the QR Code and then key in the amount. The system I will describe for you here will be even easier as your client will only need to scan your QR code.

My mobile wallet automatically shows me the approximate value of the bitcoin in US dollars (or other currency). I use that as a quick double check that I am sending about $7 not $70 or $700 because of a missed digit! That is another good reason to keep your mobile wallet balance low. You can always transfer more anytime you need it.

The very first step to getting started with bitcoin is getting a wallet. There are many choices, and you may find one is a more comfortable style than another for you. You can change wallets anytime you want, by simply transferring the bitcoin from one to another. However, if you have published bitcoin addresses (like the one above), and you delete that wallet, then any bitcoin sent to those addresses will become inaccessible.

The differences can be extremely important, and you are in no way limited to a single wallet or a single style of wallet. Except for "accounts" that may be denominated in bitcoin, any actual bitcoin wallet operates only because you have a secret code. In the absence of that code, your bitcoin is inaccessible. The owner of the wallet can't get it. Bitcoin wallets don't have an "owner" in the conventional sense of that work. Whoever has the secret code to a bitcoin address can transfer the bitcoin to another address. Whoever doesn't have the code, can't. The government can't get it. Your heirs can't get it. It is simply inaccessible. When I first wrote that, I used the word "lost", but it is not lost at all. The bitcoin exists and is ready to be transferred, but lacks only the secret code.

There are many types of wallets and exchanges. I will briefly explain the general types and some of the options. In Chapter 12. Quick Bitcoin Wallet Reviews I will describe some of the wallet apps in more detail.

Pure Bitcoin Wallet (full node)

A pure bitcoin wallet would include the entire blockchain. This type of wallet would be the most secure and also help support the distributed nature of bitcoin which is integral to its' underlying structure. The common way to get the "pure" wallet would be to download the bitcoin client from github. Once you downloaded and installed the wallet, it would then initialize and download the entire blockchain. As of Dec 2014, the blockchain is almost 30 gigabytes (something like 10 DVDs worth of data). That download will likely take numerous days, depending on your connection speed. It will also grow larger and larger.

The blockchain contains a copy of each and every bitcoin transaction that has ever taken place, starting with the very first one. That is an essential aspect of the underlying bitcoin concept.

Though I would like to recommend this option, I believe for most people it is impractical because of the installation process, data transfer and storage resources necessary. However, if you have some geek skills, there is no reason not to and it helps support the underlying distributed structure of bitcoin. You can download and install what they refer to as the "full node software": https://bitcoin.org/en/download

Web Based Bitcoin Wallet

The advantage of a web based wallet is that you don't need to install any program on your computer or cell phone. It also means you can access your wallet from any computer. BEWARE! Key capture programs and other viruses may be able to steal your passwords! For that reason seriously consider the two factor authentication options offered by most wallets. For example, Coinbase sends a code to my cell phone before I can do any transfers. Someone with my password can't initiate a transfer unless they also have my cell phone! That would make it very unlikely that a far away stranger (hacker) could access my Coinbase account. However, someone who lived in my household may not have the same difficulties!

For web based wallets, there are two kinds. One is a true wallet, for example blockchain.info. The secret keys for your wallet are yours. Although the wallet is stored on their server (and backed up to your email, cloud, pc or otherwise), the wallet is only accessible with your secret keys. Lose your password and your bitcoins are inaccessible until you can remember it. No one will be able to use them. The other kind of web-wallet, isn't a bitcoin wallet at all. It is simply an "account" denoted in bitcoin that someone else keeps in the actual bitcoin in their wallet.

There are numerous sites offering web based bitcoin wallets. Be sure to investigate them thoroughly before using one. The sign up and registration should be quick and simple. They will probably ask for an email address and that is particularly good if they do automatic backups to your email address. There should not be requests for identification information, your name (besides to show it to you when you login), ID numbers, nationality, where you live or anything else. Those offering two factor authentication will of course use a cell phone number or other means of authentication.

Bitcoin Wallet without Blockchain ("thin client")

These would be much like the "pure" bitcoin wallet but without the blockchain. Simply install the wallet and start using it. Pay particular attention to any warning about security and safety for the particular wallet you chose.

The Android wallet I have uses a simple pin code to keep people from sending money. I simply installed it from the "play store" and then sent some bitcoin to the address generated. Here you can see a screen shot of my recent transactions, balance in bitcoin and approximate value in US dollars.

That wallet required no personal information. It is available to everyone, regardless of nationality (or lack of nationality), or any banking regulations or requirements. The moment the wallet is installed, you are able to engage fully in the bitcoin economy, receiving and sending bitcoin. As I noted above in just a few minutes two friends installed the app and I sent them ten cents each. That is all it takes.

The wallets that do not download the blockchain connect to servers that provide the blockchain information, hence the name "thin client" they don't regard any large databases or downloads. This could potentially lead to security issues. These wallets are commonly used; however, keep that point in the back of your mind.

Bitcoin Accounts

Bitcoin accounts aren't bitcoin wallets at all, but are more like bank accounts. Some organization is keeping bitcoin on your behalf and gives you an account in their own system to show how much is in your account. Just as a bank may accept cash from you and in return you get account that shows how much cash you have.

Coinbase.com is a good example of this (though they are now offering optional "real" bitcoin wallets for "cold" storage of bitcoin too). If you do a transfer from your US dollar bank account to bitcoin with Coinbase, the facility will show the bitcoin in your account and allow you to transfer it to any bitcoin address. However,

21

that bitcoin is actually held by Coinbase and is under their control, not yours. Additionally if you have bitcoin sent to your account at Coinbase, it will be placed in your account there, but you have no direct access over the underlying bitcoin wallet.

For example, if you read their terms and conditions you will learn that just like with a bank account, bitcoin in your Coinbase account may be turned over to third parties when there are court orders, etc. Blockchain.info in contrast cannot do that even if they wanted to, nor any other true bitcoin wallet. The reason is that the bitcoin system is based on encryption codes. Bitcoin can only be transferred from a wallet with the proper encryption code. Without that, the bitcoin is inaccessible. With bank accounts, or bitcoin accounts, the account is simply a designation in some organization's database that you have a certain amount on deposit with them. The actual bitcoin (or in the case of bank accounts, cash), is under the control of that organization. They can for legitimate (or illegitimate) reasons transfer the bitcoin held on your behalf to someone else. They can even do so without your knowledge.

Coinbase is great for trading bitcoin to and from US, Canadian and European bank accounts, but in my view not for storing it. (Unless maybe, you look at their cold storage option.) Additionally, any organization, or exchange that gives you a bitcoin account may or may not have the underlying bitcoin available.

Just as you may worry whether a bank might actually have the cash when it comes time to make a withdrawal. As was the case with Mt. Gox. For those reasons, bitcoin accounts are best used only for short periods of time when necessary for a specific function, not as a primary means of storing bitcoin.

Bitcoin Exchanges

There are numerous bitcoin exchanges and their primary function is to exchange between bitcoin, regular currency and/or other alternative coins. Those which only exchange between virtual currencies are often open to anyone no questions asked. However, generally those who will exchange between bitcoin and regular currency, ie: US dollars, euros, etc, will require some kind of user verification.

As a stateless person who has government issued identification, I have not had any issues with the Know Your Customer (KYC) regulations at a variety of exchanges. Those without suitable identification may find it difficult if not impossible to exchange bitcoin and conventional currency through such services. Any services offering exchanges between bitcoin and regular currency without any identification requirements should be investigated so you are sure they are legit, or test them only with amounts you can afford to lose if they are not. Also, keep in mind that those types of "black market" exchanges might attract undo attention from authorities.

Like the bitcoin accounts described above, any bitcoin or currency sent to, or held by an exchange is at risk. That is why when Mt. Gox filed bankruptcy the users lost their bitcoins. The bitcoin had been in the possession of Mt. Gox, not the wallets of the individual traders. Of course, an exchange needs to run that way, or you would not be able to execute trades efficiently. It is easy to send bitcoins to your account at an exchange as well as to receive them. However, the process of sending or receiving regular currency to and from exchanges can often be slow, expensive (service charges), and/or have high limits. If you wish to play the currency markets with bitcoin, there are plenty of opportunities available, but that is not the topic of this book.

Summing Up

There are advantages and disadvantages to each kind of wallet. There is also no reason you cannot have several, one for each purpose. For example, use the exchanges for trading bitcoin, not storing it! Use a mobile wallet for using your bitcoin when you are out and about but not for storage or savings.

The site https://bitcoin.org/en/choose-your-wallet has a nice list of wallets for different platforms. You can try out several to find one that works best for you. There are also plenty choices. Be sure to search the web for reviews before entrusting one with your bitcoin. I think that you may find that the easiest way to get started with bitcoin is by installing an app on your smartphone.

If you have a bank account in their service area, Coinbase is great for transferring euros, dollars and the like in and out of bitcoin. You are never locked into one service or wallet. Remember that security and backup are very important:

-Double check bitcoin addresses and amounts before sending!

-Back up your wallet! Backups sent to your email address can be very good, if they are encrypted! You don't have to worry about losing a pen drive or your hard drive crashing.

-Passwords. Remember passwords can be grabbed by viruses. Think two factor authentication.

-Lost passwords = inaccessible bitcoin. Create a viable system of remembering and protecting your passwords.

5. Accepting Bitcoins

You've obtained your bitcoin wallet. For a quick start, I might suggest the Android, "Bitcoin Wallet". In the amount of time it takes to install the app, you can be up and running with bitcoin.

Once the app is installed, review the security instructions and set a pin code. You can then click the "request coins" button. At that point the phone will show a QR code with your bitcoin address and anyone can send bitcoin to you by scanning the QR or manually entering your address. Additionally, you can enter an optional amount and the QR code will contain both your bitcoin address and requested amount.

For example, you could scan the QR code displayed here and your wallet will immediately be prepared to send me 0.11112 bitcoins. Feel free to try it (but don't actually complete the transaction; well, on second thought, go ahead I won't mind).

With only that app and a few minutes to set it up you can start accepting bitcoin in your local business. When your client asks to pay via bitcoin, you simply click the request bitcoins button, enter in the amount, either in bitcoin or your preferred currency (though that app gives little control over exchange rates, it has an extensive list of currencies) and then display the QR code for your customer to scan.

Shortly after your customer sends the bitcoin, your wallet should indicate that it is in process. In normal circumstances that should be a sufficient indication that the transaction is OK. For large amounts, or special circumstances, you may wish to wait for one, two or more confirmations. However, each confirmation will take a minimum of ten minutes and at times much longer.

If your products or services are fairly high markup, or your main interest is to start earning and saving bitcoin, the exchange rate provided by the wallet should be sufficient for your purposes. Using it will ensure a speedy transaction without manual or confusing calculations.

You could purchase an inexpensive android phone or tablet to use exclusively for these transactions, or even use your own personal cell phone. Because a pin code is necessary to send money from the wallet, an employee can receive bitcoin without worries that they may send it somewhere else. Every so often, you could dump the bitcoin from the mobile wallet into a wallet on your PC or the web.

If you have a few friends who are also customers that have an interest in bitcoin, this is a good way to start. You could ask them to send you ten cents worth of bitcoin just to start and get a feel for the system. When I run into people with an interest in learning about bitcoin, I use a copy of the QR code from my favorite restaurant, Be Okay, and show people how I pay the check there, by sending them a "few cents." Though, now I am starting to ask people to install a wallet on their cell phone and send them a few cents directly. Having the app and a little bit of bitcoin will get them thinking and talking!

To get to the point of accepting bitcoin in your business, you didn't need to file any applications, you didn't need to show identification or signatures at the bank, and you didn't need to pay any upfront fees. There are some bitcoin transaction fees. The sender pays those and they are quite small. They are based on the amount of network data a transaction requires, not the value of it. There are no charge backs, bounced checks, or disputes. Once the bitcoin is sent, the transaction is complete.

I think for a basic point of sale (POS) application where you will manually enter the amount, using a dedicated mobile Android device will be better than using a PC, or your personal mobile phone. I recently ordered a NeuTab Model N7 (7" Android tablet with play installed) for $54.95 from Amazon.com. I think it would make a great bitcoin POS terminal. You could of course, use an iPad or more "state of the art" Android or Windows tablet, but you will receive no additional benefit.

The point-of-sale process becomes quick and easy. Print your usual cash register receipt, enter the amount into the wallet, and show your customer the QR code. They scan the code and hit the send button. Now wait a moment and see that the transaction was processed.

Keep in mind that using bitcoin puts the customer-service burden on your shoulders. The customer has no one to call for help, but you. No credit card companies to complain to. Don't use the finality of the transaction as an excuse for poor customer service or shoddy workmanship.

If your desire is simply to make some sales with bitcoin and save those bitcoins for the future, there is really nothing more you need to do. However, I would suggest setting up a PC or web-based wallet to store your coins in. Also, you could configure as many as those Android-based point-of-sale terminals as you want. You could also use iPad or Windows-based devices as well, though I have no experience with them, and the cost is likely to be much higher for no added benefit. The availability of different bitcoin wallets on Apple devices may limited as well.

However, I believe many of you will need or want to use all or part of your bitcoin revenue for your purchases, and other business or personal needs. That is, you will need to convert some of your bitcoin to your local, usable currency. You will also need to receive that currency in a form that you can use. The next sections of this book will cover a number of methods you can use to accomplish that.

My personal recommendation would be to also focus on finding suppliers to use bitcoin with. The more you can engage in bitcoin commerce, the better for the bitcoin economy. Also, if you believe there will be significant increases in the value of bitcoin over the next few years, you may look at saving as much as possible and only exchanging as much as you need, when you need it.

At this moment, bitcoin is trading for about $337. Many believe it will reach several thousand or even $10,000 in a short time. That means a $30-sale paid for with bitcoin today, could be worth $300 or even $890 in a year or two if bitcoin reaches those levels and you saved rather than spent the bitcoin.

Everything in this section has been stateless friendly, whether you have government issued identification or not.

6. The Next Step

What can you do with the bitcoin? How do you spend it? How do you go about your daily (personal or business) life in the bitcoin economy? I hope that in the near future those questions will be easy to answer. However, at this time you'll find relatively few opportunities to spend your bitcoin directly.

By following the instructions in this book, your business will be one of the first to participate in the bitcoin economy. You will help build it into a viable alternative to the conventional monetary systems that always seem to be sporting some kind of crisis if not on the brink of outright collapse. Once that bitcoin economy gets up to speed you won't have much need to go beyond what has been described above, except for greater integration of your bitcoin wallet/transactions into your cash register and accounting system.

However, because your ability to spend bitcoins directly will be at least somewhat, if not extremely limited, we need to look at practical uses that bitcoins have. There are many different ways of utilizing bitcoin right now. Depending on your circumstances and where you are located, some may be very effective and cost effective. Others may have significant fees, delays, challenges or simply be unreasonable or impossible for a variety of reasons.

Exchange with Individuals

One of the most effective way to get cash (regular currency), your local currency or another one, is by simply trading directly and personally with someone that has cash and wants bitcoin. As a small business owner who accepts bitcoin, you will be in a good position to know many people who are engaging with bitcoin. Chances are that some of them will be interested in buying more bitcoin from time to time.

That kind of transaction is as easy as making a sale with bitcoin. Meet with the person and decide on your exchange rate and what is to be exchanged. Let's assume the rate you decided on was $300 per bitcoin and the individual wanted one bitcoin. He would use his mobile wallet to request one bitcoin (or have a printed QR code with his bitcoin address). You would send one bitcoin to his account (just as your clients paid you for your products or services) and he would then pass the $300 to you.

The only challenge here is to find individuals looking to exchange bitcoin at rates you find fair and in quantities that are appropriate for you. You may run into many individuals looking to get a good exchange rate, ie: 10 or 20% better than the market rates. On the other hand you may find someone in anxious need of bitcoin for some reason and willing to pay more than market rates. You can make a decision based on your needs and the other options available.

You may also be able to help some individuals who have no interest at all in bitcoin, but instead are interested in making purchases from Amazon.com, or other internet merchants and are unable to because they don't have a suitable credit card. You could sell them an Amazon gift certificate. For example, sell them a $100 gift certificate for $100. Then purchase a $100 Amazon gift certificate from http://gyft.com with your bitcoin for them.

There is a website called http://localbitcoins.com, which is designed to be a marketplace for bitcoin transactions between individuals. It is designed for arranging personal meetings as described above as well as exchanges where the currency transfer is done via Western Union, Paypal, Bank Transfers, etc.

They also provide an escrow service (on the bitcoin side). I have used the site for transactions both in person and via Western Union. I wouldn't hesitate to recommend it for in person transactions. I also think it could be useful for buying bitcoins. However, you may well find that there are other options with better rates and lower fees.

Additionally, I believe that the use of any kind of payment that isn't definitive will open the door to many headaches. For example a payment sent via Paypal can be easily disputed by the sender. I believe there is even potential for a wire transfer to be disputed by the sender. A transaction sent via Western Union, with cash paid at an agent can't be reversed or disputed **after it is picked up**. ie: if you sell bitcoin via that kind of Western Union transfer, it is important you pick up the funds BEFORE you release the escrow. If you release the escrow when Western Union says it is ready for pickup, but before you actually pick up the funds, the other party could receive your bitcoins and then cancel the transfer!

I also believe that a Western Union transfer paid online, via credit card or bank account, could not be reversed after you picked it up. However, I strongly believe those types of transactions are ripe for fraud. Ie: someone (a hacker / criminal) via virus, trojan horse other means, obtains access to someone's credit card information or Western Union account and then uses it to buy bitcoin via localbitcoins or other means. Thus leaving, the credit card owner, the bank, Western Union or something else holding the bag. Additionally, it would likely focus interest on who received the money (you)! I have no interest in being a part of that kind of situation, knowingly or not.

For that reason, I would limit any transactions with strangers via a service like localbitcoins, to arranging a personal meeting, buying bitcoin, and/or selling your bitcoin via Western Union, Money Gram, etc, but only if you can be assured they make the payment via cash at a agent. I would look first to develop a network of local contacts interested in bitcoin.

Bitcoin Payment Services

There are a number of such bitcoin payment services. These are outstanding if you are based in the United States, Canada, and/or Europe and want a service that operates much like a credit-card merchant account. Three of the most well known services in this arena are Coinbase.com, Bitpay.com and Gocoin.com.

They are also excellent for web-based businesses. Even if their payment service aspect isn't applicable because you are not in their main service areas, they may provide a quick and effective method to add bitcoin payment to your shopping cart or website.

The focal point of these services however, is to be a payment service. You price your products or services in the currency of your choice, and when a customer checks out, or pays in person, they pay in bitcoin based on the current exchange rate of the service. The payment is sent to a bitcoin address assigned by the service (not to your bitcoin wallet). Your bank account is later deposited with the original amount and currency of your transaction.

For example, you are in the United States. You charge $100 for a product. At checkout the customer is presented with the bitcoin QR Code and a request for 0.1 bitcoins (based on that $300 exchange rate we used in an earlier example). The bitcoin is sent directly to the service and in the next day or so, $100 is deposited in your bank account.

These services work with USD, CAD and EUR and possibly other currencies and bank accounts. They also provide an option to hold back a certain percentage of the bitcoin. For example, you may select to save 1%, 10% or 50% of the bitcoin to be sent to your own bitcoin wallet and the difference as regular currency deposited in your bank account.

Gocoin also has the option to wire the currency to any bank account in the world. They didn't seem to provide any options with respect to limits, ie: only send a wire when the balance is over $5000. When I inquired, they said the wires are completed once a week. For me that is not a viable option for many small businesses outside the US, especially in markets where bitcoin use is very limited. If one received $100 in transactions during the week, the bank service charges could well exceed $50!

I think these services are exceptional for those with local businesses, websites and who also have a bank-account in one of the supported countries. The key is not where your business is located, but rather whether you have a bank account in a supported country. There is really no excuse for any business in that situation not to be accepting bitcoin now. Some large businesses including, overstock.com, expedia.com and now microsoft.com have started doing so.

Please note, you will be required to verify your identity with the bitcoin payment services. I should note that I was, as a stateless person with government issued ID to pass the verification process at the above three mentioned services.

The fees will be less than credit cards; the issue of charge backs will disappear (but read my previous note about not using that as an excuse for poor customer service), and most importantly you will be on the leading edge of technology. At minimum, I would select a 3% (or whatever you pay in credit card merchant fees) as an amount to be saved in bitcoin. Your net income would be the same and you could start amassing a stash of bitcoin.

Using these services is a good step toward bringing awareness to the marketplace. However, it is still a big step from the ultimate goal of being able to use bitcoin in all aspects of your business and personal finances as you do with currency now. Always focus on opportunities to spend bitcoin directly with your business suppliers and personal expenses.

Prepaid Credit Cards

There are a number of places that offer prepaid Visa or Mastercard cards which can be reloaded with bitcoin. I ordered three different cards from different places. I have received two of them and been using one for almost all my daily expenses since I got it. It is important when reviewing the details of the prepaid cards to examine the limits and service charges.

I have yet to find one that I think would be viable for using to fund with bitcoin and then retrieve cash at an ATM. A big part of that is because I have to pay a $5 ATM fee (local fee) to retrieve any amount of cash. The cash withdraws are usually limited to $300 or less. Plus, each card will also have its own fees. However, to make purchases, there is usually not any fee other than possible a foreign exchange fee of 1% to 3%.

ANXBTC

Anxbtc.com is a bitcoin exchange in Hong Kong. Their website is currently available in Chinese, English and Portuguese. They offer a prepaid Mastercard integrated into their bitcoin exchange. It is available in US or Hong Kong dollars. I will discuss their US dollar card.

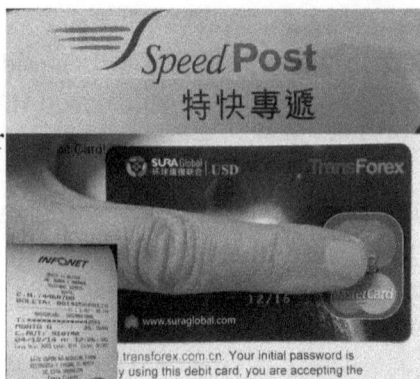

First, you will need to verify your identity with them. That means sending them a scanned government ID and a utility bill. Once you are verified you can use their exchange and order a card. I should note that being stateless with government issued ID present no problems with my verification.

The cards (or at least mine) didn't come with a name printed on it. That means you can order several and provide them to employees, or use different cards for different purposes, ie: one for business expenses and one for personal expenses.

The the time of thise writing, each card costs 0.12 BTC (that would be about US$40 at current exchange rates). Registered mail shipping costs 0.04 BTC (up to five cards), and express mail is 0.11 or 0.19 BTC depending on your location. I chose the express mail option and received my card in just over a week.

The minimum you can load on the card is $100. The maximum is $50,000. That can be confusing since you load it in bitcoin. In my experience it takes them about 12 hours to load the card. The loading is done from the Anxbtc website, or just by sending btc to the bitcoin address assigned to the card. The exchange rate they use to convert the bitcoin to US dollars seems to be about 2.5% worse than market rates. However, that is much better than many other options to get currency from bitcoin, especially without risk, hassles, or delays.

Since most of my purchases with the card are in Paraguay in guaranis and not dollars, I have another exchange rate to contend with. That is the dollars-to-guaranis when I make a purchase.

The actual Mastercard is issued by a bank in China, and after you receive the card can register on their website to manage your card. The site is in Chinese with an English version that is mostly understandable. The transaction summary provided is very nice as it provides the location of purchase, the amount in USD as well as the currency of the transaction. I found that the USD - PYG exchange rate I get with the card comes out to almost exactly the same as the local currency exchanges. This card lets me pay for almost all my personal expenses indirectly via bitcoin. For the few things that I cannot pay with the card, I could extract currency from an ATM (and suffer the high fees).

For a business, this provides the opportunity to accept bitcoin and when needed exchange it to currency for purchases. Even if your business suppliers won't accept credit cards, you could pay yourself via bitcoin and use the card for your personal purchases. This also provides you the control over how much and when you want to convert bitcoin to currency, which is not offered by the payment services.

For an initial investment of about US$150, ie: $50 for an Android table to use as a point of sale terminal and $100 for a bitcoin funded Mastercard (via express mail), you could be fully functional as a local merchant accepting bitcoin with easy exchange to USD. If you started with your own already present PC or smartphone and saved up your bitcoin until you had enough for the card, your initial investment would be exactly $0.00.

Another Card

I received a second card and it was a bit different from the one I got with some Anxbtc. At first I was extremely disappointed, but then I realized that it offers a completely different opportunity, and it may well open many doors for those outside those big three areas I keep mentioning. However, I should note that this card also says they will not ship it to, nor can be it used in a number of countries. That list is: Afghanistan, Argentina, Azerbaijan, Bolivia, Bosnia and Herzegovina, Burma, China, Colombia, Cuba, Iran, Kazakhstan,

Kosovo, Libya, Moldova, North Korea, Pakistan, Panama, Peru, Serbia, Somalia, Sudan, Syria,Turkey, Turkmenistan, Ukraine, Uzbekistan, Vietnam.

I also now read on their website that the bank is no longer issuing the card and they are only selling out the stock. The website is http://second-card.com. I am am listing it here, in case they find another source for this type of card. The cost was US$50 paid via bitcoin with gocoin as well as some other payment options in dollars.

The difference with this card is that it was not integrated at all with bitcoin. At least not directly. However, it has a European bank, IBAN number. That means that currency can be transferred to it via the swift wire transfer system or the SEPA system within Europe. In theory with that card, one could register with any of those bitcoin payment services and use that card in lieu of an actual bank account in Europe. Additionally, one could likely receive payments from others who make payments to bank accounts in Europe, likely including Paypal, Google Adsense, Amazon affiliates, etc. In fact, I configured my Amazon Kindle account to pay my royalties to the IBAN assigned to that card and within a day, received the money.

I am including the basic information on this card, because I believe there will be other similar cards made available and they provide the unique opportunity for one to engage in the European banking system from afar. I have found a number of other sources for prepaid visa cards with IBAN numbers. However, none of them I have found seem to offer a quick and simple method of ordering.

These types of prepaid cards that do not require any kind of identification are limited to a maximum loading of approximately $3,000 per year. That seems to make the $50 cost fairly high. However, they do provide an extremely useful function of providing a European bank account number.

That of course, while being a benefit to a stateless person who is unable to get any official id, also opens the door to those seeking to engage in black and/or illegal markets. Although I understand people do engage in such activities with bitcoin, as well as credit cards, cash, wire transfers and every other imaginable medium of exchange, I see the function of bitcoin as something much deeper than being another option for those kinds of markets.

I see bitcoin as a viable alternative to the failing monetary systems of the world, and possibly in the not so far future, a complete replacement for them. By engaging in the bitcoin marketplace as a normal, small business, you can help support that goal. You can help present to your customers, and those in your community that bitcoin is something much more than a tool for illegal activities.

When searching for prepaid credit card options for bitcoin, pay attention to any which provide an IBAN number. Such numbers won't interface directly with bitcoin, but will allow many bitcoin exchanges and other businesses to send money to them. You might find that is best to get one denominated in Euros, so that you avoid extra currency exchanges, as most of the places that allow you to send money, or connect to an IBAN account will only send Euros to it.

I am looking for a prepaid Visa or Mastercard with an IBAN number, which is not anonymous, that is which requires identification and doesn't have the $3,000 a year load limits. Please see my website for any updates.

Yet other cards

Many months ago, I signed up with one site that claimed to have a card in the works. I never heard anything more from them. However, a friend said he knew someone who had received their card and was using it. Another one I had ordered about two months ago, has yet to arrive. Of the three I ordered, that one had the least professional website.

You might wish to review my website for any updates on my activities in this regard and also keep an eye on bitcoin news and do Google searches.

Bitcoin exchanges

There are a number of bitcoin exchanges and some have a better reputation than others. If you are going to invest in the long term, it is better to keep your bitcoin in your own wallet and not an account at an exchange.

The purpose of this guide is not to discuss day-trading, short term or long-term investment aspects with respect to bitcoin. My focus is to present some quick and easy ways for you to participate in the bitcoin economy. My discussion of the exchanges is not from the investment perspective, but how to get dollars, euros or other "real" currency for your bitcoin when needed.

Some of the exchanges only allow trades between different virtual currencies. They often allows registration with just an email address. Others also include the abilities to exchange between bitcoin and/or other virtual currencies as well as other real currencies. These almost all require some kind of identification verification, or have very small limits for unverified users.

Additionally, each exchange provides different methods of transferring money to and from your account. There are often significant minimum transfers, service charges and time delays.

For example, as of this writing, to withdraw USD from bte-c.com the fees are: 1.5% for wire transfers (min $1,000), 7% for paypal (min $500), 1% for OKpay* (min $1). They also list some other online payment services. The wire transfer and paypal are probably the only ways to receive your US dollars in a manner allowing you to directly spend them. They claim the transfers are normally done within 72 hours. *OKpay is an online payment service, kind of like paypal, but also offers a prepaid credit card. However, they are not stateless friendly. I was unable to verify my account because "stateless" was not on their list of nationalities, and their customer service department was not particularly helpful.

A number of these online payment services, and possibly some of the bitcoin exchanges will not accept American clients. If you are American, please don't harass them by trying to evade those requirements; they are already subject to enough harassment in the financial marketplace by your government. I may soon write a commentary on how being stateless is actually beneficial compared to US citizenship and offers stateless people more opportunities and rights than enjoyed by Americans.

If you wish to go the other way and buy bitcoins with dollars, ie: deposit USD into your btc-e account, the options are much the same. However, you cannot send dollars from paypal to btc-e. The reason is simply because paypal (and credit cards) are too easy to dispute, and in such cases, would leave you with the bitcoin and btc-e, or other exchange holding the bag. Be very suspicious of any one accepting credit cards or paypal for the purchase of bitcoin. They are likely to have an extremely high rate of clients who are attempting to buy bitcoin with stolen credit cards, and/or unauthorized paypal accounts.

Coinbase does offer some ability to buy bitcoin with credit cards, but they also do verification and probably have a good collection agency to deal with those who dispute the charges.

Anxbtc, in addition to offering the prepaid Mastercard is also a full bitcoin exchange. They charge 0.5% for SEPA transfers (min 80 EUR), $25+ 0.5% for USD wire transfers (min $100), they are also connected with ZipZap in Brazil which may be worth investigating if you are in their service area. They charge 2.5% for ZipZap transfers and I believe ZipZap will only allow you to make purchases at select merchants, but not receive cash. The prepaid Mastercard seems to be a much more useful option.

There are many exchanges to chose from. It may be a good idea to register with a few and get verified so you will be ready to make use of their services when the time comes and not have to wait for the verification process.

This website has a large number of exchanges around the world listed: http://howtobuybitcoins.info. Please use common sense with respect to any of them.

7. Include Your Employees and Customers

The moment you start accepting bitcoin, you will attract a new set of customers: those who have bitcoin and are looking for places to spend it. You may well develop a whole group of regular customers simply by placing a "bitcoin accepted here" sign in your window and getting the word out.

The CEO of overstock.com said that in the first month they accepted bitcoin, "the site processed $870,000 in sales from almost 4,000 orders paid with Bitcoin."

I would encourage making a small brochure for customers, or if possible have your cash register receipt print a QR code. It could be your bitcoin address, or maybe a QR code for your website explaining your acceptance of bitcoin. It is also a good theme for a press release. Everyone who has some bitcoin in their wallet will be delighted to hear you are accepting it.

The second group to involve is your employees. Even those who aren't directly involved in your checkout process. I think a good way to include employees, is to make sure they are personally involved with bitcoin. Consider paying them a bonus in bitcoin. That will help them become familiar with the bitcoin wallet system and help spread the word!

You may even find some employees who will want a portion of their salary to be paid in bitcoin. The possibilities are endless and as you have seen with a PC, smartphone or tablet it is quick and easy to get started in the bitcoin economy. If your employees are carrying around a little bitcoin in their smartphone, you can be sure it will be a topic of discussion among their friends.

Don't forget to encourage your friends and business associates to install a bitcoin wallet on their cell phone and send them a bit or two to help them get started! You might even find a few that are interested in buying some bitcoin from you and then you are on the way to receiving bitcoin and getting cash to spend.

41

The "newness" of bitcoin is itself a selling point. There are many ways to use bitcoin now and more are coming on-line every day. Additionally, what is driving bitcoin is the sense that conventional money itself is not doing the job.

Money is a complicated phenomenon and modern money is a breathtaking experiment. It is only a century since we began expanding central banking in the West from five central banks to over 150. It is central banking

Many of these banks are coordinated out of the Bank for International Settlements in Switzerland. Thus there is a monopoly like quality to the volume and price of money around the world. Great expansions and contractions of credit continually roil markets and contract economies, causing recessions and even depressions.

Additionally, as control over money has increased, people's privacy has decreased. Banks increasingly ask intrusive questions about clients, their money and what it is meant for.

Just as questions are becoming more probing, so there are other issues emerging with banks including new policies regarding confiscation of customer assets in times of banking stress. This happened most recently in Cypress and marks the beginning of a new policy evidently. Remember with bitcoin only a person with the secret code is able to access the bitcoin.

Bitcoin has resolved many of these issues at least for now. Your bitcoin usage is not subject to overwhelming government oversight or scrutiny. So long as anonymity programs remain in place, bitcoin remains hidden from a user standpoint.

This is a driving force of bitcoin, though not one always mentioned, certainly not in mainstream media articles. But as terrorism and other justifications for government intrusions continue to expand, as doubtless they will, more and more will probably turn to bitcoin for ease of use and privacy.

8. Accepting Bitcoin and Spending, Too

If you have a web-based business, you can very quickly and easily accept bitcoin by making use of services from Coinbase, Bitpay, and/or Gocoin.

These facilities may deposit regular currency in your bank account, or pass the bitcoin onto your own wallet. They also have various options for shopping carts, integrations with common shopping carts, email invoices, etc. It will take your very little effort and add great benefit for your customers to take advantage of these resources. If you are a freelance worker and are used to sending emails to your clients with payment details via Paypal, Western Union, Xoom, etc, you could instead send them an email with your bitcoin address, QR code, or make use of one of those services to create a more professionally looking invoice by email. It will also allow you to charge in your local currency and track which clients have paid.

The focus of this guide however, is toward local businesses. Brick and mortar stores or providers of services who see their customers in person and receive payment at that moment.

I described above how you can use a basic bitcoin wallet application on your PC, smartphone or tablet to accept the payments. That is the technology. The key is of course, making it a quick and smooth process for your employees, your cashier and for your customers.

I've mentioned the restaurant that accepts bitcoin in Paraguay. When I ask for the check, the cashier prints the register receipt. Then he looks up the BTC / USD rate, then the USD / PGY rate. He converts the amount to dollars, and then to bitcoin; he writes the 8 digit bitcoin amount (for example, 0.02256564) at the bottom of the register ticket and I am presented with that and the QR code.

I then scan the QR code, key in the amount, my pin, and click send. I inform the cashier I have paid. I believe he also calls the owner to verify the payment, but that is likely done after I have left the premises.

Using the system of a basic Android tablet as a dedicated point-of-sale terminal for bitcoin, the restaurant, could print the cash register receipt, click request bitcoin, key the amount in guaranis (or their preferred currency) directly in the wallet and present the Android to me. I have a pictorial demonstration of this in Chapter 11. A Real Transaction Step-by-Step. I would then scan the QR code that included the bitcoin address and amount. That would eliminate my frustration keying in the amount, and eliminate any errors. It would be really quick, both on my end and theirs. I would simply scan the code, review the amount and click send. Additionally, their Android POS would reflect receipt of payment so the cashier could verify that I actually paid in the moment.

The one disadvantage is that the business would be forced to accept the exchange rate used by the wallet. Of course, the same basic system could be implemented on a standard PC, and the customer asked to come to the counter to check out. Keep in mind that if you are using an existing PC, the screen will need to be in a comfortable position for the customer to view and scan with his cell phone camera.

For those desiring custom exchange rates, or those able to integrate the QR code generation into their existing cash register, it may be possible include a QR code with your bitcoin address and amount on all your cash register receipts. Requiring a customer to simply scan that and send the payment.

If you are using any kind of printed QR codes instead of a live wallet, it would be wise to have an information service like blockchain.info bookmarked with your bitcoin address so you can quickly verify transactions.

In the beginning, I think unless your product or service has extremely tight margins, you would be better focused on making the process very quick and smooth for your customers and employees and not obsess too much over the exchange rate. Also, you may find that in the beginning very few customers will pay via bitcoin.

However, it is important to be ready whenever someone makes the choice.

You can be sure that those active in the bitcoin community will use word of mouth to spread their experience. I think it would be much better for your business and bitcoin to get comments like, "I paid for my lunch with bitcoin today and it was really easy", instead of something like, "I was ready to pay with bitcoin, but they said the network was down today".

As a backup you can also have a bitcoin wallet on your smartphone with a G3 connection so that if your regular internet connection really is down, you have a ready alternative. I would recommend using a wallet application on an existing PC, or a dedicated tablet. One where your cashier can simply enter the amount in your local currency and display a QR code that provides the address and amount to them. Also keep a wallet on your personal cell phone that you can use if something goes wrong with your main point-of-sale system.

Another good reason for using the exchange rate offered by your wallet is to avoid arguments over the rate you are using. It is the rate used by the XYX Wallet. Rather than ending up in an argument where a client may (mistakenly) believe you are overcharging by 5 or 10% because you are accepting bitcoin.

The Android wallet, "Bitcoin Wallet" seems to provide all the functionality and a good list of currencies. In five minutes you can have that installed and be accepting bitcoin. Remember to set a pin code on that wallet so others can't send bitcoin from it, and setup another wallet on your PC or that is web based, that you regularly transfer your proceeds too.

I would recommend starting simple and keeping it simple. You really have no excuse for not hanging a "Bitcoin accepted here" sign on your door today.

Spending Bitcoin Online

There are many opportunities to spend your bitcoin online. For customers and merchants it is much quicker, easier and cost effective than using a credit card. With bitcoin you can easily make purchases from Amazon.com. Although Amazon doesn't accept bitcoin, you can buy a gift certificate for Amazon with bitcoin.

I did my Christmas shopping that way. I bought a $500 gift certificate from gyft.com, paid for it with bitcoin, and then it was applied to my Amazon account. It was quick, easy and without any hassles. You can buy Amazon gift certificates ranging from $10 to $2,000.

You may also find that this is a method you can use to get cash for your bitcoin. You may have a customer who wants to make a purchase from Amazon, but is unable to because they don't have a credit card which is acceptable to Amazon.com. You could sell them a $100 Amazon Gift certificate for $100 and then purchase that certificate with your bitcoin. Gyft is currently offering a bonus for gift certificates paid for with bitcoin, so you can get a really good deal.

Many other websites are now starting to accept bitcoin, for example, overstock.com, microsoft.com, expedia.com (at least for certain travel services). There are also numerous small businesses that accept bitcoin. The list is growing everyday. As a local business accepting bitcoin, you'll be able to immediately use it for online purchases at any of these merchants.

9. Safety and Security

Bitcoin has some aspects that are similar to cash, but it also much different. If you send bitcoin, it is much like giving someone cash. There is no way to get it back. It also has some aspects of cash. You need only obtain a wallet ... a computer application, or in some cases a computer generated address printed on paper.

That wallet and the bitcoin addresses in it aren't directly associated you with as a person. That doesn't mean it is impossible for someone to make a connection between a wallet and the person in charge of it. However, on the other side all transactions are public. All transactions, since the very first one, are stored on the "blockchain" and a copy is kept on many computers across the world.

Some websites, such as blockchain.info allow anyone to examine any bitcoin transaction from the very beginning. They have various options to search by transaction id, bitcoin address, etc.

One of the reasons for using a new bitcoin address for every transaction is to help maintain your privacy. Anyone in the world can see the transactions that any bitcoin address has sent or received. However, there is no direct means to see exactly which addresses are held in a specific wallet.

Each address is made up of two encryption codes. One is public and is used to transfer bitcoin to that address. The other is secret and is used to transfer bitcoin from that address. You can easily see the importance of the secret code. With it, anyone can transfer bitcoin from your address. Without it, not even you can transfer your own bitcoin. Because those encryption codes are long and difficult to remember, it is normal for them to be stored in an encrypted form in your wallet. Your wallet then uses a password that you select to protect the real encryption codes.

That password and making effective backups of your wallet then become of key importance. Additional factors to consider: How someone can access your bitcoin if you are not available, ie: sick, injured, or passed away. Unlike traditional finances where they may have legal avenues available for access to your assets, bitcoin provides the technological issue, that your coins are encrypted and unavailable without the password.

Traditional means of protecting information, ie: guarding your passwords in a safe, safety deposit box, lawyers office, etc would all be suitable for making your bitcoin assets available in those kinds of situations. However, it also means that your bitcoins are only as safe as that information. For more protection, you could entrust a part of the password with a lawyer and another part of it in a safe deposit box. Thus, someone would need access to both the lawyers files and safety deposit box to access your bitcoin. Here are a few points to consider:

Good Passwords

A good password is one that you can easily remember, as well as one that is not easily guessed or calculated by others. Using digits, 0-9, characters @#$%, Upper and lower case letters is always recommended. Additionally, many websites, and wallets offer two factor authentication. This requires your password and another verification that you are you. For example, many send a code via text message to your cell phone. This of course doesn't verify that you are you, but only the user accessing your account knows your password and has your cell phone at the moment.

This type of two factor authentication is excellent protection against far away strangers (hackers) who might get your password by means of a virus or phishing attack or other means. They would not have your cell phone, and thus be unable to access your account.

It is also a very good idea not to use the same password for your email, and bitcoin wallet. If you have multiple bitcoin wallets, again, it is best to use a different password for each one. It would be a good idea to develop a good way to keep track of your different passwords. I know there are programs designed to help you store all your passwords under one password. I'm not sure this is effective as anyone who could access that password vault would have access to all your passwords!

Multiple Wallets

I think for many reasons you will want to use multiple bitcoin wallets. Most importantly, you will want to keep most of your bitcoin on your PC or in a web based wallet, and send small amounts to your mobile wallet for day to day purchases. Any wallet that your employees have access to in the process of accepting bitcoin in your business, you'll want to empty daily (or after any large transaction) so you have no worries about problems there.

You may also want to to use different wallets for different purposes. One for your long term savings, one for your general expenses, your mobile wallet, your wallet to receive bitcoin. Of course, as you start out, I would recommend two wallets. One on your PC (or web based) and one on your bitcoin point of sale terminal.

Good backups

Each different wallet app will its' own method of backing up the data. These backups should be encrypted with password protection. That means if someone gets a copy of your backup, it won't give them access to your data without the password. In the case of backups, I don't believe there are any two factor authentication options available.

Some web wallets, such as blockchain.info can be set to automatically do a backup after every transaction. They can send those backups to your email, cloud account, hard drive, etc. It is important to regularly backup your wallet. You could potentially lose access to some of the bitcoins in your wallet if your hard drive crashes (pc based wallet). For mobile wallets the risk is likely higher due to the ease of breakage, loss or theft of those devices.

In the case of mobile devices, there are two risks. One is that whoever finds your device could send the coins, and the second is that you would lose the wallet information and access to the bitcoin.

A good pin or password for the wallet should stop others from access your coins. A good, regular backup means you can simply restore your wallet on another device and have full access. In the case of a lost or stolen device, I would immediately restore your wallet and then transfer all your bitcoin from it, to another wallet (just in case someone can figure out your pin or password). I would then start with a new wallet installation and new bitcoin addresses. I would only restore the old wallet for the purpose of transferring the bitcoin out of it.

Often you can chose how to backup your wallet, to your hard drive, to the "cloud", to your email, to a pen drive, etc. For a web based wallet, you may consider doing backups to your email and hard drive. Your email, is probably a good place for wallet backups since it is away from your house, business, computer, etc. Also, it is probably free, so you don't have to worry that your backup will be deleted if you miss a payment!

If your wallet has an option for automatic backups, I would take advantage of that. If not, get in the habit of making regular backups!

Some wallets also offer the option of a paper backup. Be extremely careful with these as they may not be encrypted meaning that anyone who see the paper can access your bitcoins. Additionally, if you do make such a paper backup, be sure you securely destory the paper when it is no longer of use to you.

Someone who finds such a backup in the trash may well be able to access your bitcoin well into the future! Additionally, don't present the paper in a manner by which it may be recorded or broadcast by video systems, be it a CCTV security system or a television interview! Someone could press pause and scan the QR codes with your secret codes!

10. Frequently Asked Questions

Q: Do I need to be online to accept bitcoin?

The person who is sending bitcoin to you must be connected to the Internet. It would be a good idea to offer free wifi in the area where customers will be paying with bitcoin. Otherwise, only those who have cellular based internet will be able to make a purchase with bitcoin.

If you present your customers with a printed QR code, there is no requirement that you be online in order to receive it. However, it would be a good idea so you can verify the transaction went through. Also, unless your products or services are priced in bitcoin, you will likely need to be online to calculate the exchange rate.

By offering free wifi in your checkout area, and using an Android tablet as your point of sale device, you can complete the transactions very simply and little worries about internet connectivity for you or your clients.

If you do not have an internet connection or wifi router, most cell phones all you to easily configure a wifi base so that others can tether to your cell. That would be a viable method of offering wifi for your clients to pay with bitcoin.

Q: What if the value of bitcoin drops?

The variation in exchange rates, particularly the decline of the value of bitcoin is of concern. That is one of the reasons many merchants try to exchange all their bitcoin for currency as soon as possible. Depending on where you are located, that may not be possible. It is a risk you take. Of course, with other payment options there are risks. You have the risk of charge backs with credit cards, where you could lose the merchandise, the payment and pay a hefty service charge to the bank. With cash you have the risk of robbery or receipt of counterfeit cash. With checks you have to deal with bounced and stolen checks.

I believe the constant exchange of bitcoin to currency by the services such as Bitpay, Coinbase and Gocoin keeps a study flow of bitcoin on the marketplace and consequently lower prices. As more become engaged in the bitcoin to bitcoin economy without the constant exchange to currency, I believe will result in the opposite effect, a pressure toward increasing exchange rates.

Q: What if the value of bitcoin increases?

Many believe that bitcoin will inherently increase in value because of it is a limited resource. Only the future will tell, but perhaps the best strategy is to save as much bitcoin as possible and only spend what is absolutely necessary. In the short term of course, there will be fluctuations. I believe, however, over the long term we will see a trend upwards and that will happen as more become engaged in the bitcoin economy.

Q: How do I keep my bitcoin secure?

Review the section on safety and security, focus on good passwords, regular backups, two factor authentication, and also making use of multiple wallets (don't keep all your eggs in one basket).

Q: What are the benefits of accepting bitcoin?

Your are opening your business to a whole new group of customers: people with bitcoin. You are starting to participate in a new economic system, the cost to get started is low and you can be on the leading edge, not trying to play catch-up.

Q: What devices can I use for a point of sale terminal?

You can use any device that has a bitcoin wallet available for it. My preference is to use a low-cost Android tablet (make sure it comes with the Play Store pre-installed), however, most any Smartphone, tablet, iPad, iPhone or other internet connected device should work. A regular PC, or even a QR code printed on a piece of paper is sufficient.

In the most basic form, without any internet access, you could have a friend open a wallet for you and print a QR code with your address on it. Just be sure you have the password for the wallet and not your friend. Your customers could scan that printed code and send bitcoin to your wallet.

Q: What if I have a problem?

One of the challenges of working with a new technology, and engaging with a new economic is where to go when you need help. This is especially true with bitcoin where there is no central service or business that is in charge of it. There is no merchant agreement like with credit cards, so neither you, nor your customers have an outside customer service agent to call.

However, I think you will find that the bitcoin wallets operate exceptionally well. It is a technology based system, that is not dependent on human interactions as with bank transfers, etc. The key is being sure the bitcoin address and amount is 100% correct before you send it.

Most of your problems will probably be when someone sends the wrong amount, or the correct amount more than once. You'll need to work out your customer service procedures for those situations. It is also a keep idea to keep up to date on bitcoin related news and when a real problem appears, spend some time researching for answers.

Local bitcoin user groups and other stores accepting bitcoin would be good to network with. Also, keep a list of your trusted bitcoin clients handy.

11. A Real Transaction Step-by-Step

This chapter will overview a complete bitcoin transaction from start to finish. It will use a basic Android tablet a Nuetab Model N7 which I purchased on Amazon.com for $54.95 as the point of sale terminal. I will use my LG cell phone as the customer.

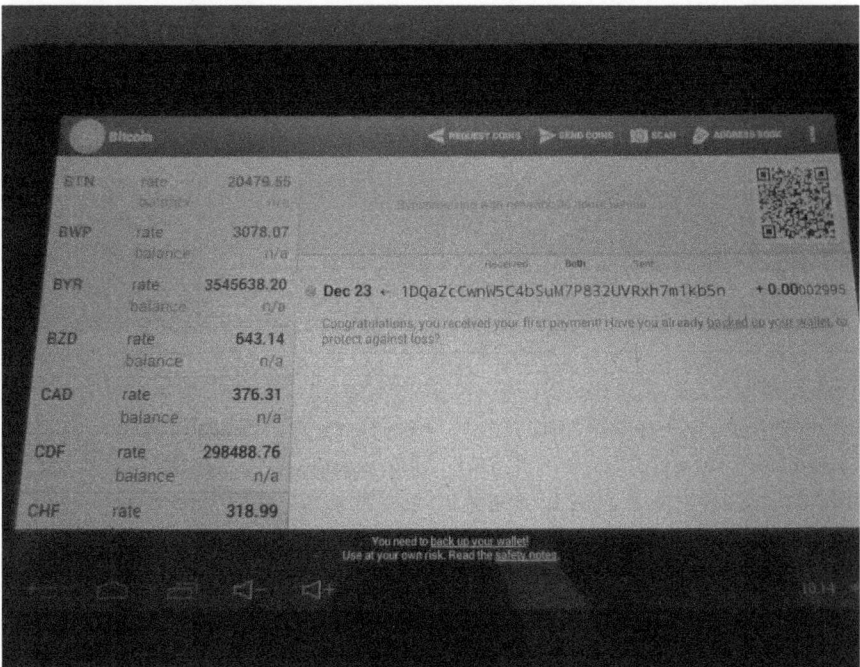

This image shows the list of currencies the Bitcoin Wallet can use. It shows the approximate exchange rate for each currency and lets you select one as your default. Your balance is shown in bitcoin along with the approximate value in the selected currency. When you send bitcoin, or ask to receive it, you can enter the amount in either bitcoin or the selected currency. I set the default currency on the tablet to Paraguayan Guaranis. On my cell phone, it is set to US dollars.

The home screen of the bitcoin wallet shows the wallet balance, approximately 1 cent from when I was testing yesterday. Here, I touch the request bitcoins button. That is how you would begin the bitcoin transaction. Just like with a credit card sale, you would prepare your cash register ticket. However, instead of swiping the credit card and keying in the amount, you would touch the request bitcoin button.

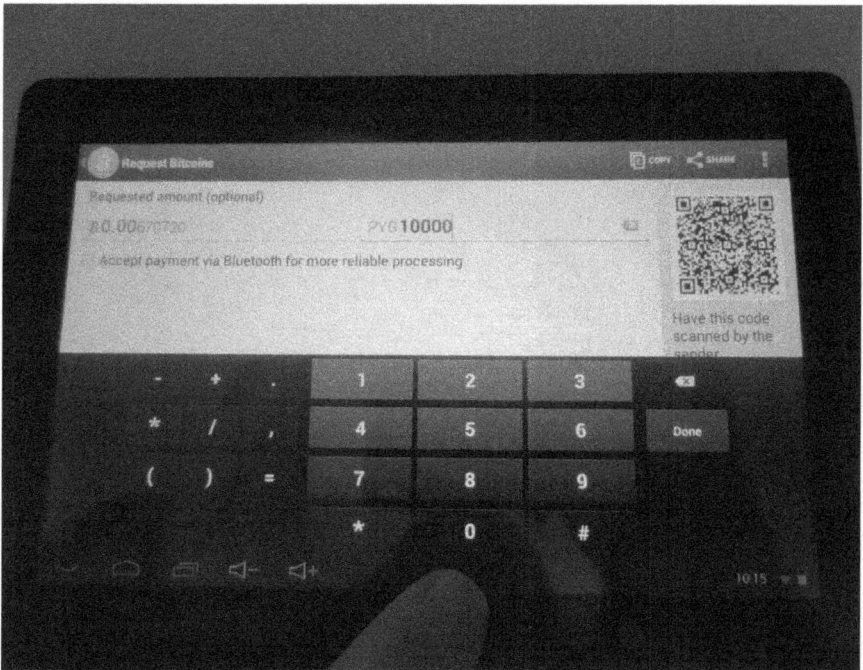

After touching request bitcoin, I can enter an amount in bitcoin or the default currency, in this case Paraguayan guaranis. I enter 10,000 guaranis. It automatically calculates the amount in bitcoin (see my previous discussion about exchange rates). If no amount is entered, the QR code will only contain your bitcoin address and your customer will need to manually enter an amount. As the amount is entered a small QR code in the corner of the screen contains the address and amount. You might actually see this code changing as you enter in the amount and the code is updated.

I touch the small QR Code and it is displayed in a larger, easier to scan format. Now the transaction is ready to be paid by your customer.

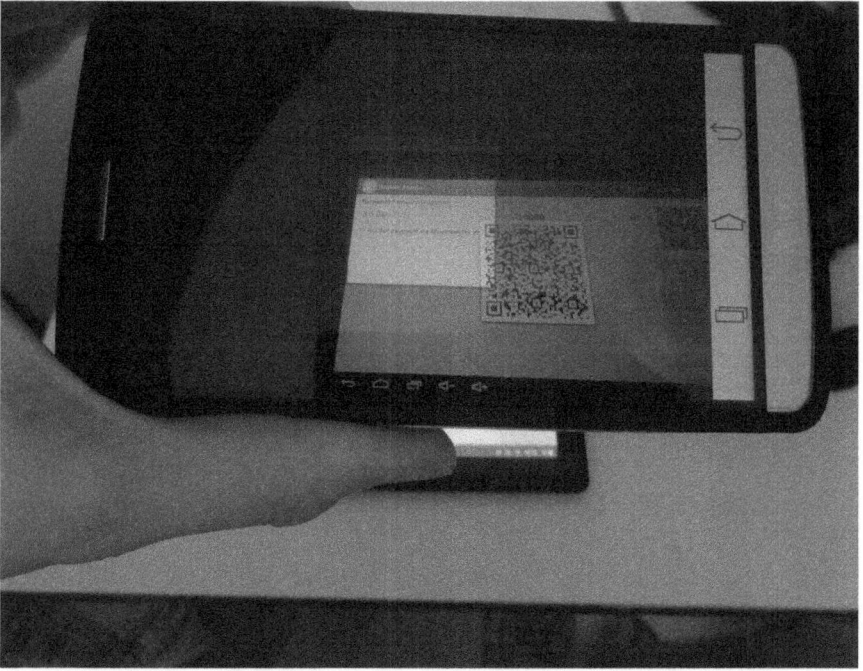

On my cell phone (the customer) I click send bitcoin and then click the camera icon to indicate I will be scanning a QR Code. The white square section on my screen is the area it will scan for a QR code. I move my camera so that the QR code fits within that square. The moment the QR code is recognized, the scanning is complete.

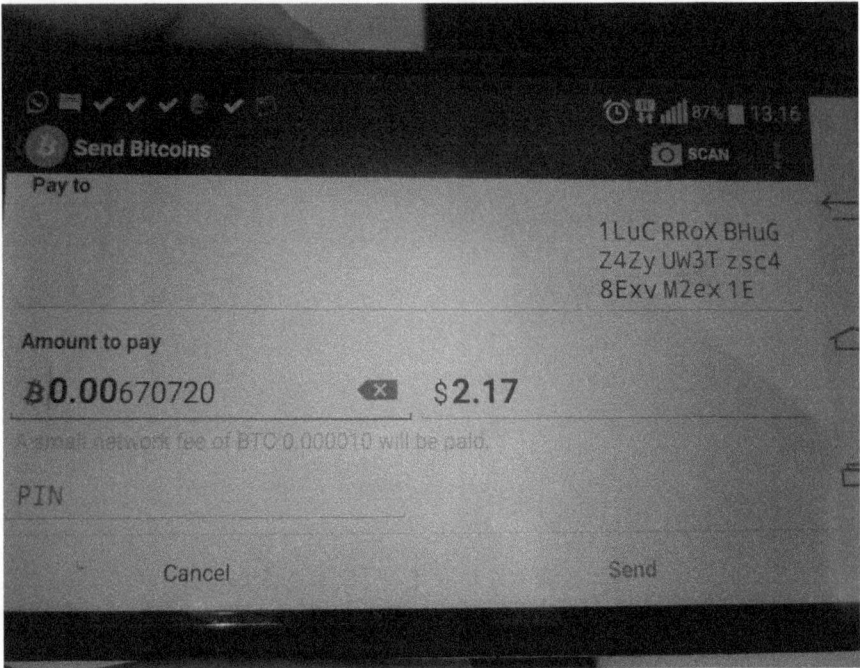

Pay to

1 LuC RRoX BHuG
Z4Zy UW3T zsc4
8Exv M2ex 1E

Amount to pay

B0.00670720   ✕ $2.17

A small network fee of BTC 0.000010 will be paid.

PIN

Cancel   Send

My cell phone (the customer) now shows the bitcoin address to send to (from the QR code) and the amount in bitcoin and in this case approximate value in US dollars because that is the currency I have selected on my wallet. Incidentally, if I divide 10,000 by 2.17 I get 4608 which is very close to the exchange rate I would get at the local currency exchange. To complete the transaction, I need to enter my pin code, which I do now.

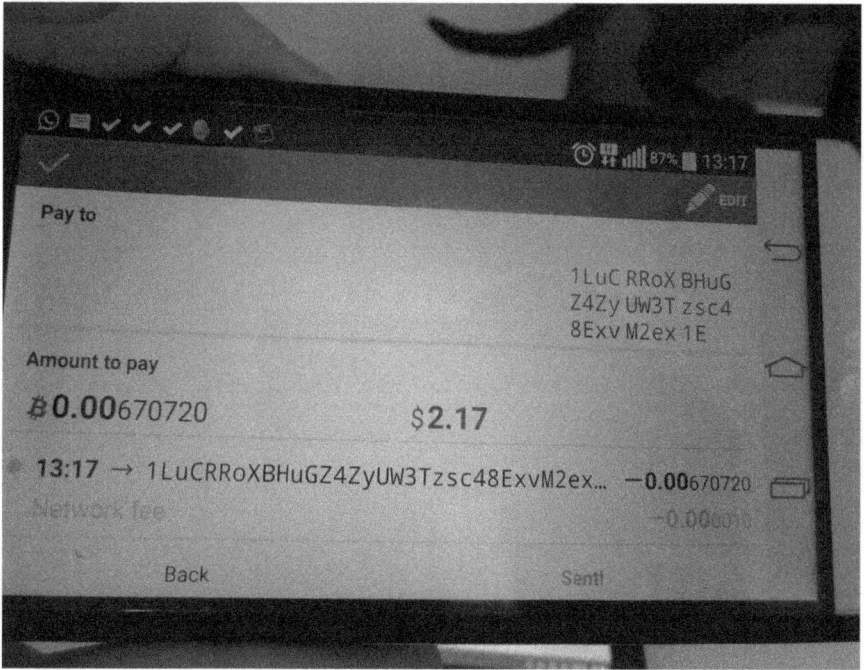

My cell phone now shows a summary of the transaction and that the status is "sending", a moment later the status changes to "sent" and my tablet (which received the bitcoin) will beep.

Now, back to the tablet (your bitcoin point of sale terminal) and we see the transaction is received. As I've talked about in this book, that bitcoin is now "stored in your tablet*." For that reason, it is important to have a suitable pin code set so that an unauthorized employee or customer can't transfer the bitcoin out of your tablet. Additionally, it would be a good idea once a day, or after any significant transaction to transfer the bitcoin to a more secure wallet.

The process of accepting bitcoin from a customer is no more complicated than the steps outlined above. Request bitcoin, key in the amount (in bitcoin or the currency of your choice), show your client the QR code. Your customer scans the QR code and completes the payment with a couple touches of the screen of their smartphone.

You will probably find that a bitcoin transaction done this way is faster than swiping a credit card and presenting the receipt for your customer to sign.

* All transactions are actually stored in all full nodes of the bitcoin network, not in your actual devices. Your bitcoin wallet contains only the public and secret encryption codes to access your bitcoin.

12. Quick Bitcoin Wallet Reviews

I will present a quick review of four different bitcoin wallets. Two are PC based and two are Android based. There are many wallets and your final decision should be based on what you find works best for you.

My recommendation to start with is for MultiBit on your PC and Bitcoin Wallet for Android.

Electrum PC

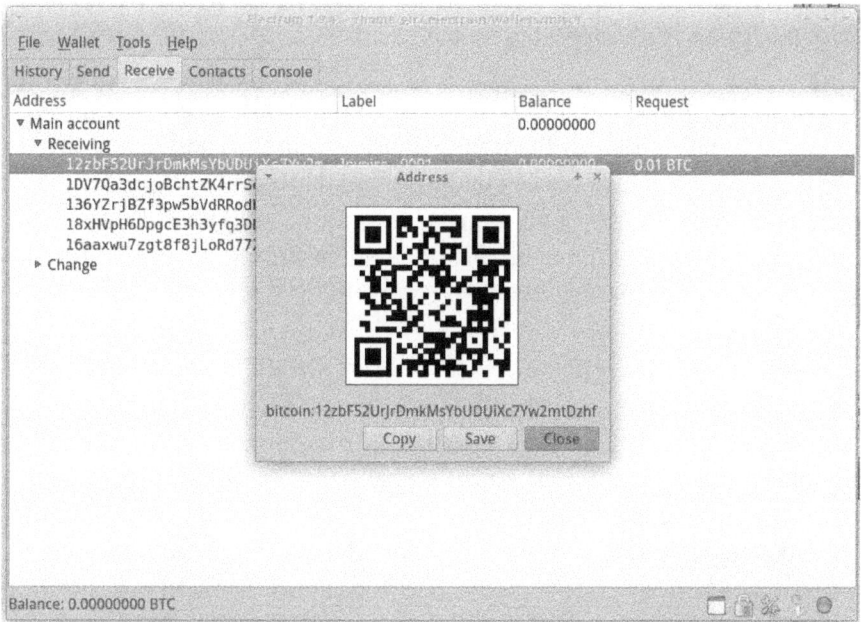

Electrum for the PC (Linux version 1.9.4). The installation was quick and easy. However, it generated a "default wallet" which was passport protected and I was never prompted for the password or told what it was. I believe this could be extremely dangerous as any bitcoin I may have sent to the wallet would have been thereafter inaccessible by me! Always test new wallets with small amounts of bitcoin to make sure you can send and receive without any issues

I created a new wallet and was prompted for a password. I was also given a list of code words to save (you must save them as you will be prompted to enter them again). These code words can be used to restore the wallet if you forget the your password. Anyone else with these code words can access bitcoin stored in that wallet.

This is a clean, basic bitcoin wallet. Although the "plugins" menu has an option for currency exchange and euros, selecting that seems to have no effect. ie: this is straight bitcoin. Additionally, the QR code for requesting coins provided just the bitcoin address and not the amount.

There does not seem to be a built in option for backing up your wallet. Make sure you determine where it is located on your PC and regularly back it up. Also view the notes below from Electrum about why a backup is unnecessary!

For your PC, I think this may be an excellent wallet for storing your bitcoins, receiving them from your POS terminal(s) and sending them to other services for exchanging, etc. Unless you have an efficient means to calculate your BTC amounts and want your customers to be scanning the QR code and entering the BTC amount by hand, I do not recommend it for your POS.

You can create multiple wallets and easily switch between them using File / Open. Additionally, you can send bitcoins to multiple addresses by creating a .CSV file listing addresses and amount of bitcoin to sent to each one. For example, if you wanted to give each of your employees a weekly bitcoin bonus, you could create a simple spreadsheet in Excel with their bitcoin addresses and the amounts. It would then be very quick to send the bonuses. Double check your addresses and amounts!

Electrum's website says: "Electrum is an easy to use Bitcoin wallet. It protects you from losing coins in a backup mistake or computer failure, because your wallet can be recovered from a secret phrase that you can write on paper or learn by heart. There is no waiting time when you start the client, because it does not download the Bitcoin blockchain." https://electrum.org

Additionally, and explaining some of my installation issues of their Android version: "Ubiquitous: You can use the same wallet on different computers, they will synchronize automatically." However, my desire is to have an independent wallet on my cell phone and my PC. I want my cell phone wallet to have only a small quantity of bitcoins stored on it.

The Android version of Electrum seems not to be a fully functional wallet, but simply a mirror of your PC wallet allowing you to see your balance and any deposits.

I would pass on Electrum for any mobile or point of sale operations, but would consider it for a general bitcoin wallet on your PC. The ease of creating and switching between wallets is a great feature.

MultiBit PC

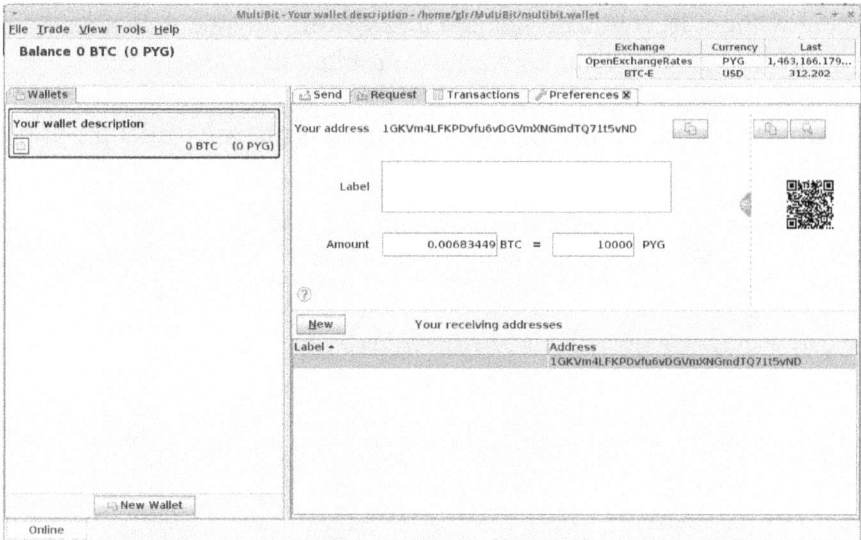

MultiBit is an easy to use PC based wallet that offers a number of currency exchange options. If you select "OpenExchangeRates", you can select most any currency of the world. Including Paraguayan Guaranis. However, you will have to register with the Open Exchange Rates page, and copy and paste your "App ID". This is not difficult and adds great functionality to the wallet. However, Open

Exchange Rates allows only 1,000 rate queries per month, or about 33 a day, once per hour.

They also allow a second exchange rate to be shown. The wallet will display updated BTC exchange rates in the two selected currencies. They will allow you to enter either bitcoins or the first selected currency when sending or requesting bitcoin.

That makes it a viable wallet to use as a point of sale terminal. You can enter the amount of your sale in your local currency and then your customer can scan the QR code which includes the bitcoin address and amount. The transaction will then appear on the Transaction screen so you can verify receipt it of.

You can easily add additional wallets for other purposes. Remember to use File / Add Password to each wallet so your bitcoins cannot be spent without it! If you do not add a password, anyone with access to your computer will be able to send your bitcoin!

I would recommend MultiBit as a verstile easy to use wallet for your PC.

This is really a quick and simply wallet to install, configure and used. There is really no configuration necessary, except for setting a pin code, selecting a default currency for exchange rates. You can also select if you want BTC values show as bitcoin, mbtc, ubtc, etc. I personally find the mbtc and ubtc setttings to be extremely confusing. They refer to milli and micro btc. A shifting of the decimal point by 3 or 4 places.

Bitcoin Wallet defaults to mbtc and I would immediately change it to btc to avoid confusion. I would always use straight bitcoin, ie: 0.00000001 and double check via the exchange rate. ie, if you are trying to send $7 and key in (or scan) 0.23 btc instead of 0.023 then exchange rate would show about $70!

Please review the section under "safety" with regards to backing up your wallet and do so regularly! Make sure to use a secure password for your backup and remember it. You can easily email your backups to any email address. Best one that is not accessible via your cell phone.

I highly recommend this wallet for use as a quick and easy point of sale (POS) terminal for your business. You can set your local currency as the default and quickly create QR codes with your bitcoin address and amount for your customers to scan.

Although I didn't see what languages Bitcoin Wallet is available in, it seems to use your default Android language. On my cell it operates in English, on a friends cell it appeared in Spanish.

I would highly recommend Bitcoin Wallet for Android as an excellent wallet to start with. It is quick and easy to install and you can be trading bitcoin with your friends in just minutes to learn the ropes. It also makes a great point of sale terminal.

Green Address Android

Green Address is a bit more complicated to configure than Bitcoin Wallet. It also requires you to set up a two factor authentication system. However, using email or SMS which is received by your cell phone seems to kinda defeats the purpose.

Green Address also offers some exchange rates, but their list of currencies is much smaller than with Bitcoin Wallet. However, you can select different Bitcoin exchanges for some of the currencies, for example with USD you can select Bitstamp, btc-e, localbitcoins among other options. It also offers a variety of languages including English and Spanish.

The screens seem more cluttered than with Bitcoin Wallet, but more options are available. I think this can be a serious contender when you are looking for more security and options. However, I would start with Bitcoin Wallet.

13. Conclusion

In this book we've discussed what bitcoin is and how to set up a bitcoin wallet and go into business using bitcoin. The information I've provided here can be utilized by friends and family as well as customers.

It is important to remember, as you create an awareness about bitcoin that this is more than simply another transactional offering. Bitcoin is truly a revolutionary money in terms of how it works and the promise that it offers to users.

Bitcoin provides anonymity, privacy and low transaction fees at a time when mainstream money is becoming increasingly onerous and transparent.

One does not have to be involved in questionable activities to want to preserve privacy in this day and age and bitcoin offers that promise.

One should also recall in the past that when governments are stressed, as they are today, inflation tends to rise along with taxes. If governments are truly stressed they may engage in overt confiscation of assets. This confiscation can involve pensions, retirement income, social security and other payment streams due the retiree.

Worst case, bank accounts can be frozen and confiscated as they were in Cypress not long ago. The idea there is that savers are in a sense unsecured lenders of the bank and therefore their savings are actually bank assets and subject to confiscation.

For purposes of portability, ease-of-use, privacy and safety, bitcoin provides users with solutions not available anywhere else.

14. Contact Information

The author is not available for personal consultations. However, you are welcome to share your comments with him. Please note any emails sent may be published on his site and/or used in future articles, books, and/or other media.

bitcoinbus@glr.com

Mr. Roberts also has a website to provide news, commentary and interviews on topics related to bitcoin: http://profitbitcoin.com He will also use that site to provide updates to the topics covered here: http://profitbitcoin.com/ct/20 (English) or http://es.profitbitcoin.com/ct/1f (español).

His personal website is: http://GlenLeeRoberts.me Twitter: @GlenLeeRoberts

The PDF version of this book may be purchased with Bitcoin at: http://www.nimblewisdom.com

Media inquiries can be directed to: mediax@glr.com

The author did not receive any compensation for any of the services described in this book. They were selected based on his personal experiences. Nothing should be considered an endorsement of any product or service. Bitcoin is a new technology and should be used at your own risk.

Please consult your attorney and/or accountant for any legal and accounting advice with respect to legal and tax issues.

www.ingramcontent.com/pod-product-compliance
Lightning Source LLC
Chambersburg PA
CBHW032016190326
41520CB00007B/500